The R.A.C.E. Is On!

A Step-by-Step Writing Guide for Elementary Students

Yvonne McCowen, Ed.D.

The R.A.C.E. Is On!

Copyright © 2025 by Dr. Yvonne McCowen

All rights reserved. No parts of this publication may be reproduced, distributed, or transmitted in any form or by any means, including photocopying, recording, or other electronic or mechanical methods, without the written permission of the publisher, except in the case of brief quotations embodied in critical reviews and certain other noncommercial uses permitted by copyright laws. Unless otherwise indicated.

Transitions Publishing

Missouri City, TX 77459

Preface

During my more than twenty years of teaching I've encountered thousands of students who find it difficult to master the essential skill of writing clear and thoughtful answers to questions. Many young writers struggle to express their thoughts in writing during reading comprehension tests, class discussions and simple homework assignments.

Students used to write one-word answers, and they would frequently go off on completely unrelated tangents. I dedicated countless hours to writing comments such as "Great idea!" My students and I both experienced genuine frustration when I had to write notes like "But where's your evidence?" and "You're on the right track—explain more!" Then, I discovered the **R.A.C.E.** method, and everything changed.

The **R.A.C.E.** writing strategy provides students with an uncomplicated, organized method to structure their thoughts effectively and boost their writing confidence while enabling them to answer questions fully. Through four straightforward steps of **Restate, Answer, Cite, Explain** students develop the ability to create responses which demonstrate clarity and depth while being well-supported.

R.A.C.E. not only enhances test results and homework performance but also instills foundational life abilities, teaches essential life skills:

- ✅ Critical thinking involves teaching students to substantiate their ideas with concrete evidence.

- ✅ Clear communication requires expressing thoughts in a logical sequence while maintaining proper structure.

☑ Writing confidence emerges when students understand precisely what they want to communicate and how best to express their thoughts.

The guide aims to make mastering and applying the **R.A.C.E.** approach a straightforward and beneficial experience. The **R.A.C.E.** method provides an engaging and accessible learning experience while delivering effective results for students, parents, and educators alike. The guide includes detailed explanations along with examples and activities plus troubleshooting advice that support writers at every skill level to learn this technique.

Throughout my career I have observed the direct impact of **R.A.C.E.** on student writing skills. The **R.A.C.E.** method helps students develop from timid one-sentence responders into self-assured writers who analyze content. After implementing this approach, you will witness young learners develop the ability to express themselves clearly while thinking critically and writing purposefully.

Yvonne McCowen Ed.D

Veteran Educator | 20+ Years in the Classroom

Table of Contents

Introduction 1

Chapter 1: Understanding the R.A.C.E. Method 4

Chapter 2: Step 1 - Restate the Question 8

Chapter 3: Step 2 - Answer the Question 13

Chapter 4: Step 3 - Cite Evidence 21

Chapter 5: Step 4 - Explain Your Answer 27

Chapter 6: Applying the R.A.C.E. Method 34

Chapter 7: Common Mistakes When Using the R.A.C.E. Method & How to Fix Them 40

Chapter 8: Fun Activities to Reinforce Learning 47

Chapter 9: Fiction & Nonfiction Reading Passages and Writing Prompts 53

About the Author 64

Bibliography 65

Introduction

Writing is an essential skill for students, and the R.A.C.E. method provides a structured approach to answering questions with clear and complete responses. R.A.C.E. stands for Restate, Answer, Cite, and Explain. This method helps young writers develop critical thinking skills, organize their thoughts, and improve their writing clarity. In this book, we will outline each step of the R.A.C.E. method and provide practical examples and activities to reinforce learning.

Writing is more than just a skill—it's a **critical foundation for learning**. Research consistently shows that students who develop strong writing abilities early on perform better across subjects, from **reading comprehension** to **math problem-solving** (Graham & Hebert, 2011). However, national assessments such as the **NAEP (National Assessment of Educational Progress) Writing Report** reveal that a significant number of elementary students struggle with **constructing complete, well-supported written responses** (National Center for Education Statistics, 2012).

Many students fall into one of these common writing pitfalls:

✘ **Providing vague, one-sentence answers** without explanation.

✘ **Going off-topic or misunderstanding the question.**

✘ **Failing to use evidence** from the text to support their answers.

✘ **Lacking structure** in their responses, making them difficult to follow.

Educators and literacy experts emphasize that **explicit, structured instruction** in writing is essential to helping young learners build confidence and competency (Shanahan, 2016). This is where the **R.A.C.E. method** comes in.

The **R.A.C.E. method** is a **four-step strategy** that helps students develop complete, well-organized responses to questions about a text. It breaks writing down into **manageable, easy-to-follow steps**:

◆ **Restate** the question in a statement form.

◆ **Answer** the question clearly and concisely.

◆ **Cite** evidence from the text to support the answer.

◆ **Explain** how the evidence proves the answer.

By following this structured process, students learn how to:

✅ **Organize their thoughts logically** rather than writing random details.

✅ **Support their answers with evidence**, improving comprehension skills.

✅ **Write in complete sentences**, a critical skill for all academic subjects.

✅ **Build confidence in their responses**, leading to better test performance and classroom engagement.

For many young writers, formulating a response can feel overwhelming. The **R.A.C.E. method simplifies the process**, giving them a clear **roadmap** to follow. Research on **scaffolding in writing instruction** (Pea, 2004) suggests that providing structured steps helps students bridge the gap between basic responses and more advanced analytical writing.

Additionally, the R.A.C.E. method:

✏️ **Aligns with Common Core, Texas TEKS, and other writing standards**, which emphasize text-based evidence.

✏️ **Encourages critical thinking**, an essential 21st-century skill.

✏️ **Supports struggling writers** by giving them a step-by-step process to follow.

✏️ **Helps ELL (English Language Learner) students** organize their thoughts and build academic language skills.

When used consistently, the **R.A.C.E.** method becomes second nature to students, **improving their writing performance across all subjects**.

The **R.A.C.E.** method is most effective when answering **text-dependent questions**, but it can also be applied to:

✏️ **Reading comprehension questions**

✏️ **Short constructed responses on tests**

✏️ **Essay writing in upper elementary grades**

✏️ **Science and social studies written explanations**

By using the **R.A.C.E.** method in daily writing practice, students develop the habit of **thinking critically, structuring their answers clearly, and using evidence effectively**—skills that will benefit them throughout their education.

Now that we understand why the **R.A.C.E.** method is such a valuable tool, we'll explore each step in detail in the following chapters. Through **practical examples, engaging activities, and guided practice**, students will gain the skills they need to become **stronger, more confident writers**.   Let's get started! 🚀

Chapter 1: Understanding the R.A.C.E. Method

- Overview of the R.A.C.E. method
- Why it is useful for elementary students
- When to use the R.A.C.E. strategy in writing assignments

Overview of the R.A.C.E. Method

The R.A.C.E. method is a structured writing strategy designed to help elementary students craft clear, complete, and well-supported responses to questions. It is especially useful for answering reading comprehension and essay questions in a way that ensures students stay focused and provide thorough explanations.

R.A.C.E. stands for:

- **Restate** the question: Students begin their response by turning the question into a statement, ensuring clarity and focus.
- **Answer** the question: They provide a direct response, making sure to address all parts of the question.
- **Cite** evidence: Using supporting details from the text, students reinforce their answer with factual evidence.
- **Explain** their reasoning: They connect their evidence to their answer, elaborating on why it supports their response.

This method helps young writers organize their thoughts, strengthen their comprehension skills, and develop critical thinking. By practicing the R.A.C.E. method, students learn to provide well-structured and insightful written responses, improving both their academic performance and confidence in writing.

The **R.A.C.E. method** is useful for elementary students because it provides a **structured, step-by-step approach** to writing clear and complete responses. Here's why it's beneficial:

1. **Builds Writing Confidence** – Many young students struggle with organizing their thoughts. The R.A.C.E. method gives them a clear formula to follow, making writing feel less overwhelming.

2. **Encourages Complete Answers** – Instead of writing short or vague responses, students learn to fully answer a question with supporting details and explanations.

3. **Improves Reading Comprehension** – By requiring students to **cite evidence** from the text, this method reinforces careful reading and helps them understand how to support their ideas with facts.

4. **Develops Critical Thinking Skills** – The **explain** step encourages students to think beyond the text, making connections and analyzing why their evidence supports their answer.

5. **Prepares for Standardized Testing** – Many standardized tests require written responses. The R.A.C.E. method helps students practice constructing well-organized, evidence-based answers, a skill they will use throughout their education.

6. **Teaches Good Writing Habits** – By consistently using this structured method, students develop essential writing skills that will benefit them in

    future essays, research projects, and real-world communication.

Overall, the **R.A.C.E. method** simplifies writing for elementary students, helping them become more effective and confident writers!

The **R.A.C.E. strategy** is best used in writing assignments that require **structured, evidence-based responses**. Here are the ideal situations for using this method:

1. **Reading Comprehension Questions** – When students answer questions about a story, article, or passage, the R.A.C.E. method ensures they respond thoroughly and use **text evidence** to support their answers.

2. **Short-Answer and Extended Responses** – This method is particularly helpful for **constructed response questions** on tests, quizzes, and homework assignments. It helps students organize their answers clearly and completely.

3. **Opinion and Persuasive Writing** – If a prompt asks students to share an opinion (e.g., "Do you think the main character made the right choice?"), the **Cite** and **Explain** steps help them provide evidence and reasoning for their viewpoint.

4. **Science and Social Studies Assignments** – The R.A.C.E. method can be used beyond reading and language arts! In subjects like **science** and **social studies**, students can use it to support answers with facts from textbooks, articles, or classroom discussions.

5. **Test and Exam Prep** – Standardized tests often require written responses. Practicing the R.A.C.E. method helps students develop strong habits for structuring their answers under time constraints.

6. **Writing Summaries and Book Reports** – When summarizing a book or article, students can use **Restate** to introduce the main idea, **Answer** key questions about the content, **Cite** examples from the text, and **Explain** how those details support their summary.

By using the **R.A.C.E. method** in these writing tasks, students develop a habit of thinking critically, organizing their thoughts, and writing more effectively!

Chapter 2:
Step 1 - Restate the Question

- What does it mean to restate?
- The importance of turning a question into a statement
- Examples and guided practice activities

What Does It Mean to Restate?

Restating means **rewording** the question in a way that turns it into a statement to begin a response. This step ensures that students clearly show they understand the question and stay focused on answering it.

Why Is Restating Important?

- It helps **clarify** the topic of the response.
- It ensures students **stay on topic** and answer what is being asked.
- It makes writing **more structured and professional** rather than just jumping into an answer.

How to Restate a Question

To restate, students should:

1. **Remove the question words** (who, what, when, where, why, how).
2. **Rearrange** the words into a statement.
3. **Use key words** from the question to stay on topic.

Examples of Restating a Question

✅ **Question:** *Why is the main character brave?*

✅ **Restated:** *The main character is brave because...*

☑ **Question:** *What is the theme of the story?*

☑ **Restated:** *The theme of the story is…*

☑ **Question:** *How does the author show the setting?*

☑ **Restated:** *The author shows the setting by…*

Encouraging students to **always start with a restated statement** helps them develop strong writing habits and makes their responses clearer!

The Importance of Turning a Question into a Statement

Restating a question as a statement is a crucial first step in the **R.A.C.E. method** because it helps students **organize their thoughts, stay on topic, and create strong, structured responses**. Here's why it matters:

1. Ensures Clarity

Restating the question **sets the stage** for a clear and focused answer. It helps the writer, and the reader understand exactly what is being addressed.

☑ **Example:**

Question: *Why is friendship important in the story?*

Restated Statement: *Friendship is important in the story because…*

By starting with a restated statement, the response stays **clear and direct**.

2. Helps Students Stay on Topic

When students restate the question, they are less likely to **go off-topic** or provide an incomplete response. It acts as a **guide** to keep them focused on answering what is asked.

3. Makes Responses Sound More Professional

Instead of **jumping straight into an answer**, restating **creates a complete thought** and makes writing sound polished and academic.

✅ **Example:**

Weak Response: *Because she helped her friend when she was sad.*

Strong Response (with restating): *The main character is kind because she helped her friend when she was sad.*

4. Prepares Students for Higher-Level Writing

Restating teaches students how to **begin essays and short responses in a structured way**, preparing them for **more advanced writing** in later grades.

By turning questions into statements, students build strong **writing habits** that improve both their confidence and the quality of their work!

Examples & Practice for Restating Questions

Here are some examples and practice activities to help students master the **Restate** step in the R.A.C.E. method.

◆ Examples of Restating Questions

✅ **Example 1:**

Question: *Why is teamwork important in the story?*

Restated: *Teamwork is important in the story because...*

✅ **Example 2:**

Question: *How does the main character show kindness?*

Restated: *The main character shows kindness by...*

✅ **Example 3:**

Question: *What lesson does the story teach?*

Restated: *The story teaches the lesson that…*

✅ Example 4:

Question: *What is the setting of the story?*

Restated: *The setting of the story is…*

✅ Example 5:

Question: *How does the author create suspense?*

Restated: *The author creates suspense by…*

📝 Practice Activity: Restate the Questions

Instructions: Rewrite each question as a statement.

1. Why is honesty an important theme in the book?
2. How does the character solve the problem?
3. What is the main idea of the passage?
4. Why do you think the author chose this title?
5. How does the story's setting affect the plot?

(Encourage students to write their responses in complete sentences using the R.A.C.E. method!) 😊

Notes

Chapter 3:
Step 2 - Answer the Question

- How to directly answer the question
- Avoiding off-topic responses
- Examples of strong and weak answers

How to Directly Answer a Question

After **restating** the question, the next step in the **R.A.C.E. method** is to provide a **direct answer**. This means giving a **clear and specific response** that addresses all parts of the question.

◆ Steps to Answer a Question Directly

1. **Use the Restated Question as a Guide**
   - Your answer should connect **directly** to the restated question.

2. **Be Concise but Complete**
   - Provide the main answer **without adding unnecessary details** at this stage.

3. **Make Sure Your Answer is Correct**
   - Use knowledge from the text, lesson, or topic to provide an **accurate** response.

✓ Examples of Answering Directly

Example 1:

Question: *Why is teamwork important in the story?*

Restated: *Teamwork is important in the story because...*

Direct Answer: *...it helps the characters solve problems and support each other.*

Example 2:

Question: *How does the main character show kindness?*

Restated: *The main character shows kindness by...*

Direct Answer: *...helping others and sharing with friends.*

Example 3:

Question: *What is the theme of the story?*

Restated: *The theme of the story is...*

Direct Answer: *...the importance of friendship and trust.*

📝 Practice Activity: Answer the Questions Directly

Instructions: Restate and answer each question clearly.

1. Why is honesty an important theme in the book?
2. How does the character solve the problem?
3. What is the main idea of the passage?
4. Why do you think the author chose this title?
5. How does the story's setting affect the plot?

Once students master **directly answering**, they can move to the **Cite Evidence** step to support their response! 😊

How to Avoid Off-Topic Responses

One of the biggest challenges for students when writing is staying **focused** and **on-topic**. In the **R.A.C.E. method**, the **Answer** step must directly relate to the question. Here's how to avoid straying off-topic:

◆ Tips for Staying on Topic

1. **Read the Question Carefully**
   - Make sure you **understand what is being asked** before writing your response.
   - Identify **keywords** in the question (e.g., "Why," "How," "Explain").

2. **Restate the Question Properly**
   - If the question is restated correctly, it will guide the answer in the right direction.

3. **Answer Only What is Asked**
   - Avoid adding extra details that **do not relate** to the question.
   - **Example:** If asked about the **theme** of a story, do not describe the **plot** unless it directly supports your answer.

4. **Use Text Evidence to Stay Focused**
   - If an answer is based on **facts from the text**, it is less likely to go off-topic.

5. **Check Your Work**
   - After writing, **reread your response** and ask:
     - *Did I fully answer the question?*
     - *Did I include unnecessary details?*
     - *Does my response make sense?*

✅ Example: Staying On-Topic vs. Off-Topic

Question: *How does the main character show bravery?*

✗ Off-Topic Answer:

"The main character has a dog named Max and loves playing outside. One time, she climbed a tree and saw a bird."

(*This does not answer the question about bravery!*)

✅ On-Topic Answer:

"The main character shows bravery when she stands up to the villain and protects her friend, even though she is afraid."

(*This answer stays focused on bravery and directly answers the question.*)

📝 Practice: Identify and Fix Off-Topic Responses

Instructions: Read each response and decide if it stays on-topic or goes off-topic. If it's off-topic, rewrite it to make it more relevant.

1. **Question:** Why is friendship important in the story?
   - **Response:** The story takes place in a small town during the winter. The main character loves playing in the snow.

2. **Question:** How does the author create suspense in the story?
   - **Response:** The author creates suspense by using cliffhangers and describing intense action scenes in detail.

3. **Question:** What lesson does the main character learn?
   - **Response:** The main character learns to always be honest because lying can hurt others. Also, her favorite food is pizza.

Examples of Strong and Weak Answers

A **strong answer** is clear, direct, and fully answers the question, while a **weak answer** is vague, incomplete, or off topic. Below are examples of to help students recognize the difference.

◆ Example 1: Question & Response

Question: *Why is teamwork important in the story?*

✕ Weak Answer:

"Because they work together."

(This answer is too vague. It does not explain how teamwork is important or provide details from the story.)

✓ Strong Answer:

"Teamwork is important in the story because it helps the characters solve a difficult problem. For example, when they worked together to build a bridge, they were able to cross the river safely."

(This answer is specific, explains why teamwork matters, and includes an example.)

◆ Example 2: Question & Response

Question: *How does the main character show kindness?*

✕ Weak Answer:

"She is nice to people."

(This answer does not provide enough detail or a specific example.)

✓ Strong Answer:

"The main character shows kindness by helping her friend when she is hurt. For example, she stays with her and brings her a bandage to make sure she is okay."

(This answer clearly explains how the character is kind and gives a specific example.)

◈ Example 3: Question & Response

Question: *What is the theme of the story?*

✘ Weak Answer:

"The theme is to be happy."

(This answer is too broad and does not explain why this is the theme.)

☑ Strong Answer:

"The theme of the story is that friendship is important. The story shows this when the main character learns to rely on her friends for help and support during a difficult time."

(This answer clearly states the theme and provides reasoning from the story.)

◈ Quick Checklist for a Strong Answer:

- ✔ **Restates** the question
- ✔ **Directly answers** the question
- ✔ **Includes details or examples**
- ✔ **Is clear and specific**

📝 Practice: Fix the Weak Answers

Instructions: Read the weak answers below. Rewrite them to make them strong by adding details and examples.

1. **Question:** What lesson does the main character learn?
    - **Weak Answer:** *She learns a lesson about honesty.*
    - **Your Strong Answer:** _____

2. **Question:** How does the setting affect the story?
   - **Weak Answer:** *The setting is in a forest.*
   - **Your Strong Answer:** _____
3. **Question:** Why did the author choose this title?
   - **Weak Answer:** *Because it fits the story.*
   - **Your Strong Answer:** _____

Notes

Chapter 4:
Step 3 - Cite Evidence

- What is citing evidence?
- How to find supporting details in a text
- Sentence starters for citing evidence
- Practice exercises with short reading passages

What is Citing Evidence?

Citing evidence means providing **specific details** from a text or source to support your answer or claim. In the context of the **R.A.C.E. method**, **Cite** refers to using facts, quotes, or examples from the reading or the lesson to **back up** the answer you provided.

Citing evidence is an important step because it shows that your response is based on **facts** or **specific information**, not just your opinion or general knowledge. It strengthens your answer and makes it more **credible**.

◈ Why is Citing Evidence Important?

1. **Supports Your Answer:**
2. Evidence helps explain **why** your answer is correct, making your response stronger and more reliable.
3. **Shows Understanding:**
4. Citing evidence demonstrates that you have read and understood the text, not just skimmed it.
5. **Builds Credibility:**
6. By citing specific examples from the text, you prove that your response is grounded in the material, rather than being a vague or unsupported guess.

✅ Example of Citing Evidence in the R.A.C.E. Method

Question: *Why is teamwork important in the story?*

Restated Question: *Teamwork is important in the story because...*

Direct Answer: *Teamwork is important because it helps the characters achieve their goals.*

Cite Evidence: *For example, when the characters worked together to build a shelter, they were able to stay safe during the storm. The text says, "Together, they built a strong shelter that could withstand the heavy rain."*

Explanation: *This shows that teamwork was essential for their survival, as they needed each other's skills to complete the task successfully.*

◆ How to Cite Evidence Properly

1. **Find Specific Examples or Quotes:**
2. Look for direct quotes, actions, or specific moments from the text that support your answer.
3. **Use Proper Phrasing:**
4. Use phrases like:
    - *For example, the text states...*
    - *According to the author...*
    - *In the story, it says...*
5. **Avoid Over-quoting:**
6. Use just enough of the quote or example to make your point. You don't need to copy large sections; a few words or sentences are enough.

📝 Practice: Cite Evidence

Instructions: For each question, write a direct answer and then cite evidence from the text or story to support your answer.

1. **Question:** How does the main character show bravery?
    - **Your Direct Answer:** _____
    - **Cite Evidence:** _____

2. **Question:** What lesson does the story teach?
    - **Your Direct Answer:** _____
    - **Cite Evidence:** _____

3. **Question:** Why is friendship important in the story?
    - **Your Direct Answer:** _____
    - **Cite Evidence:** _____

Here are a few **short practice passages** with questions to help students practice citing evidence. The passages are designed to be easy to read and provide opportunities for using the **R.A.C.E. method** (Restate, Answer, Cite, Explain).

Passage 1:

Passage:

Lily loved to spend time in the garden. One day, while picking flowers, she saw a butterfly struggling in a spider's web. Lily gently freed the butterfly and watched it fly away. She felt proud of herself for helping the little creature.

Question:

How does Lily show kindness in this passage?

Your Direct Answer: _____

Cite Evidence: _____

Explanation: _____

Passage 2:

Passage:

Jake was nervous about the big race, but his friends encouraged him. "You can do it, Jake!" they shouted. With their support, Jake felt braver. When the race began, he ran faster than he ever had before and finished in first place.

Question:

How does teamwork help Jake in the race?

Your Direct Answer: _____

Cite Evidence: _____

Explanation: _____

Passage 3:

Passage:

The storm came quickly. The trees swayed in the wind, and the rain came down in sheets. But the people in the town worked together to help each other. They helped secure homes, share supplies, and make sure everyone was safe.

Question:

What role does teamwork play during the storm?

Your Direct Answer: _____

Cite Evidence: _____

Explanation: _____

Passage 4:

Passage:

Mia was excited to visit the zoo. She saw many animals, but her favorite was the giraffe. "Look at how tall it is!" Mia said. She watched the giraffe carefully, amazed at how it could reach high branches with its long neck.

Question:

What does Mia learn about giraffes?

Your Direct Answer: _____

Cite Evidence: _____

Explanation: _____

Passage 5:

Passage:

The sun set over the ocean, and Sarah sat quietly on the beach. She felt calm as she listened to the sound of the waves. It was the perfect end to a busy day.

Question:

How does the setting affect Sarah's feelings?

Your Direct Answer: _____

Cite Evidence: _____

Explanation: _____

Feel free to use these passages in practice or to have students write their own answers using the **R.A.C.E. method!** ☺

Notes

Chapter 5:
Step 4 - Explain Your Answer

- Why explaining matters
- Connecting evidence to the answer
- Using transition words and phrases
- Sample explanations and student-friendly templates

Why Does Explaining Your Answer Matter?

The **explanation** step in the **R.A.C.E. method** is crucial because it helps students **clarify their thinking, deepen their understanding**, and demonstrate why their answer makes sense. Here are a few key reasons why **explaining** your answer is so important:

◆ 1. Shows Critical Thinking

Explaining your answer forces you to think beyond just stating a fact. It helps you analyze **why** something is true, how it connects to other ideas, or why it's important. This is a valuable skill that builds **critical thinking** and **problem-solving** abilities.

Example:

If you say the main character is brave, explaining why helps you reflect on specific actions or behaviors that prove this bravery.

◆ 2. Strengthens Your Argument

An explanation **adds depth** to your answer. It's not just about saying something is true but providing a clear **reason or justification** for why it's true. Without explanation, your answer can seem shallow or unsupported.

Example:

If you say "The theme of the story is friendship," explaining why (e.g., "The characters always help each other and share their feelings") shows you understand the theme deeply.

◆ 3. Helps Clarify Your Thoughts

The **explanation** step allows you to **organize your thoughts** and ensure your answer makes sense. It's easy to give a quick, surface-level response, but explaining your answer helps you ensure you've considered all aspects of the question.

Example:

If you say, "The setting affects the story," explaining how the setting creates tension or impacts the characters' choices helps you organize and structure your answer clearly.

◆ 4. Improves Communication Skills

Explaining an answer teaches you how to clearly and effectively communicate your ideas. In both academic settings and real-world situations, being able to explain why you believe something is important to others.

Example:

In group discussions or writing, explaining your ideas encourages others to understand your point of view and builds stronger, more thoughtful conversations.

◆ 5. Helps with Assessments and Test Responses

In many assessments and tests, **explaining** your answer demonstrates to teachers or evaluators that you can back up your response with evidence, logic, and understanding. Simply providing an answer without explanation might not fully capture your knowledge.

Example:

If you are answering a multiple-part question on a test, giving a detailed explanation can help you earn more points because it shows that you **understand** the material, not just memorize it.

📝 Example of Explaining Your Answer in Action:

Question: *Why is teamwork important in the story?*

Direct Answer: *Teamwork is important because it helps the characters accomplish tasks they couldn't do alone.*

Cite Evidence: *In the story, when the group worked together to build the bridge, they were able to cross the river safely.*

Explanation: *This shows that when the characters combined their efforts, they could overcome challenges that would have been impossible to face individually. Teamwork made them stronger and more successful.*

Conclusion:

Explaining your answer is important because it makes your response more **complete, logical**, and **persuasive**. It's not just about having the right answer; it's about being able to **articulate why** that answer makes sense and supporting it with clear reasoning.

What Types of Transition Words Should Be Used and Why?

Transition words are essential in writing because they **connect ideas smoothly**, making responses clearer and easier to follow. In the **R.A.C.E. method**, transitions help **move from one part of the response to the next**—from restating, to answering, to citing evidence, to explaining.

◆ Types of Transition Words and How to Use Them

1. Transitions for Restating the Question

Use these words to introduce your restated question:

- **In other words,**
- **To put it another way,**
- **This means that...**

✓ Example:

Question: Why is teamwork important in the story?

Restate with Transition: *In other words, teamwork is important because it helps the characters solve problems together.*

2. Transitions for Answering the Question

Use these to **introduce your direct answer** clearly:

- **The main reason is...**
- **One way is...**
- **It is important because...**

✓ Example:

"One way teamwork is important is that it helps the characters build a safe shelter during the storm."

3. Transitions for Citing Evidence

Use these to smoothly introduce **proof from the text**:

- **For example,**
- **According to the text,**
- **The author states,**
- **In the passage, it says,**
- **The text explains,**

✅ Example:

"For example, the text states, 'Together, they built a strong shelter that could withstand the heavy rain.'"

4. Transitions for Explaining Your Answer

Use these to **clarify how the evidence supports your answer**:

- **This proves that...**
- **This shows that...**
- **This means that...**
- **As a result,**
- **Because of this,**

✅ Example:

"This shows that teamwork was necessary for survival, as they needed to combine their efforts to stay safe."

◆ Why Are Transition Words Important?

✔ **They make writing flow better**

✔ **They help connect ideas smoothly**

✔ **They make responses clearer and more organized**

✔ **They show relationships between ideas (cause/effect, examples, etc.)**

📝 Practice: Fill in the Missing Transitions

1. **Question:** How does the character show kindness?
    - The character shows kindness by helping her friend. _____, when her friend was sad, she cheered her up. _____, kindness is an important theme in the story.

2. **Question:** What lesson does the main character learn?
    - The main character learns to never give up. _____, he fails at first but keeps trying. _____, he finally succeeds, showing determination is key. 😊

Notes

Chapter 6
Applying the R.A.C.E. Method

- Step-by-step practice activities
- Guided writing prompts
- Sample responses using the R.A.C.E. strategy

Activities, Prompts, and Responses to Apply the R.A.C.E. Method

Here are some **fun and effective activities** that help students practice the **R.A.C.E. method** (Restate, Answer, Cite, Explain). These activities include **writing prompts, discussion exercises, and hands-on engagement strategies** to reinforce learning.

Writing Activities

1. "R.A.C.E. Response Challenge"

☑ **How it works:**

- Write several **short reading passages** (fiction or nonfiction).
- Provide **a question for each passage**.
- Students use the **R.A.C.E. method** to write a complete response.
- Challenge students to highlight or underline each part:
    - 🔵 **Restate** in blue
    - 🟢 **Answer** in green
    - 🟡 **Cite** in yellow
    - 🔴 **Explain** in red

💡 Example Passage & Question:

Passage: *Liam practiced every day for the soccer championship. Even when he felt tired, he kept training. On game day, his hard work paid off when he scored the winning goal.*

Question: *How does Liam show determination?*

✅ Strong R.A.C.E. Response:

Restate & Answer: *Liam shows determination by never giving up on his soccer training.*

Cite Evidence: *For example, the text says, "Even when he felt tired, he kept training."*

Explain: *This shows that Liam was committed to improving and did not let obstacles stop him.*

2. "R.A.C.E. Partner Share"

✅ How it works:

- Pair students up.
- Give them a **writing prompt** and a **short passage**.
- One student writes the **R** and **A** (Restate & Answer).
- The other student writes the **C** and **E** (Cite & Explain).
- They switch and review each other's responses for clarity and accuracy.

💡 Prompt Example:

"How does the main character show bravery in the story?"

✏️ Speaking & Discussion Activities

3. "R.A.C.E. Around the Room"

✅ How it works:

- Post **four large posters** in different corners of the room, labeled **R, A, C, and E**.
- Give students a **question based on a reading passage**.
- Students move to each station and contribute a part of the response.
- At the end, they piece together a full answer using the R.A.C.E. method.

💡 Example Question:

"Why is honesty an important theme in the story?"

4. "Hot Seat R.A.C.E."

✅ How it works:

- One student sits in the "Hot Seat."
- The teacher asks a question about a story or topic.
- The student must respond using the **R.A.C.E. method out loud**.
- The class listens and provides feedback on whether all parts were included.

💡 Example:

"How does the setting impact the events in the story?"

🎮 Interactive & Hands-On Activities

5. "R.A.C.E. Puzzle Pieces"

✅ How it works:

- Write **four parts of a response** (Restate, Answer, Cite, Explain) on separate puzzle pieces.
- Mix up the pieces and have students **match them together correctly**.
- This helps reinforce the **structure** of the method.

💡 Example Puzzle:

Question: *What is the main theme of the story?*

- Piece 1: *The main theme of the story is kindness.*
- Piece 2: *For example, the text says, "The boy helped the stranger carry her groceries even though he didn't know her."*
- Piece 3: *This shows that kindness means helping others, even when you don't have to.*
- Piece 4: *Kindness is important because it makes the world a better place.*

6. "R.A.C.E. Dice Roll"

✅ How it works:

- Give students a **die with 6 sides**, each labeled with different R.A.C.E. tasks (e.g., **R, A, C, E, Fix an Answer, Swap with a Friend**).
- Students roll and complete that part of the response for a given question.
- If they land on **"Fix an Answer,"** they must improve a weak response.

- If they land on **"Swap with a Friend,"** they switch papers and check each other's work.

💡 Example Question:

"How does the author build suspense in the story?"

🎨 Creative Writing Prompts

7. "What Would You Do?" (Personal Response)

✅ How it works:

- Ask students real-life scenario questions.
- They must use the **R.A.C.E. method** to respond with **logical reasoning and evidence from their experiences**.

💡 Example Prompts:

1. *Why is it important to be a good friend?*
2. *How can hard work help you achieve your goals?*
3. *Why should students read every day?*

✅ Example R.A.C.E. Response:

Restate & Answer: *Being a good friend is important because it helps build strong relationships.*

Cite Evidence: *For example, when my friend was sad, I helped cheer her up, and she felt better.*

Explain: *This shows that friends should support each other in both good and bad times.*

8. "R.A.C.E. Comic Strip"

✅ How it works:

- Have students create a **4-panel comic strip**.
- Each panel represents a step in the **R.A.C.E. method**.

- They write a short **response and drawing** for each part.

💡 Example Question:

"How does the character solve a problem in the story?"

📌 **Panel 1:** Restate & Answer

📌 **Panel 2:** Cite Evidence

📌 **Panel 3:** Explain

📌 **Panel 4:** Show the Conclusion

Conclusion & Takeaways

The **R.A.C.E. method** is an excellent way to **improve writing structure**, **develop strong responses**, and **help students become better thinkers**. These activities make learning **engaging and interactive** while reinforcing the importance of **Restating, Answering, Citing, and Explaining**.

Mastering the **R.A.C.E. method** can help elementary students become stronger, more confident writers. By practicing these steps regularly, students will learn to write more structured and well-supported responses. Encourage students to use this method in their writing, and they will be on their way to success!

Chapter 7
Common Mistakes When Using the R.A.C.E. Method & How to Fix Them

While the **R.A.C.E. method** is a great strategy for structuring responses, students often make **common mistakes** that can weaken their answers. Below are **key mistakes** along with tips on how to fix them.

🛑 1. Skipping the Restate Step (R)

🔎 **Mistake:** Some students **jump straight to answering** the question without restating it in their own words.

✅ **How to Fix It:**

- Remind students that restating the question **helps clarify their response**.
- Teach them to **turn the question into a statement**.
- Provide sentence starters like:
    - *The main idea of this passage is…*
    - *One reason why ___ is important is…*

💡 **Example:**

✘ *"She was brave because she saved the cat."*

✔ *"The character showed bravery when she saved the cat from the tree."*

2. Giving an Incomplete or Vague Answer (A)

Mistake: Students may **not fully answer** the question or give a vague response.

How to Fix It:
- Have students **underline key words** in the question to make sure they fully answer it.
- Encourage them to be **specific** and **detailed**.
- Use sentence starters such as:
  - *One way ___ is shown in the story is…*
  - *The main reason why ___ happened is…*

Example:

✗ *"The main character is brave."*

✓ *"The main character is brave because she faced her fear and entered the dark cave."*

3. Not Citing Evidence Properly (C)

Mistake: Some students either **don't include text evidence** or **don't introduce it properly**.

How to Fix It:
- Teach students to **introduce their evidence** with a phrase like:
  - *For example, the text states…*
  - *According to the passage…*
  - *The author writes…*

- Remind them that evidence **must come directly from the text**—not just their own opinion.
- Have students practice highlighting **where they found their evidence** in the passage before writing their response.

💡 **Example:**

✗ *"She is brave because she went into the cave."*

✓ *"For example, the text states, 'Even though she was afraid, she stepped into the dark cave to find her lost dog.'"*

🛑 4. Explaining Poorly or Not Explaining at All (E)

🔍 **Mistake:** Students may **state evidence without explaining** how it supports their answer.

✅ **How to Fix It:**

- Teach students to ask **"Why does this evidence matter?"**
- Encourage them to **connect their evidence to the main point**.
- Provide sentence starters like:
    - *This shows that…*
    - *This proves that…*
    - *As a result, we can see that…*

💡 **Example:**

✗ *"For example, the text says, 'She stepped into the cave.'"*

✓ *"For example, the text states, 'She stepped into the cave.' This proves that she is brave because she overcame her fear to help someone in need."*

⬣ 5. Using Off-Topic or Irrelevant Evidence

🔴 **Mistake:** Some students pick **random text evidence** that **doesn't actually support** their answer.

✅ **How to Fix It:**

- Teach students to **double-check that their evidence matches their answer**.
- Have them explain **why the evidence is relevant** before writing it down.
- Practice with **multiple pieces of evidence** and ask:
    - *Which one best supports your answer?*
    - *How does this prove your point?*

💡 **Example:**

✗ *"For example, the text says, 'The dog wagged its tail happily.'"* (This doesn't prove bravery.)

✔ *"For example, the text says, 'She entered the cave even though she was scared.' This proves she is brave because she took a risk to save her pet."*

⬣ 6. Writing in a List Instead of Connecting Ideas

🔴 **Mistake:** Some students treat the R.A.C.E. method like **a checklist** without smoothly transitioning between ideas.

✅ **How to Fix It:**

- Teach students to **use transition words** to connect ideas:
    - *Because of this...*

- As a result...
- This proves that...

- Have them **read their response out loud**—if it sounds robotic, they need smoother connections.

💡 Example:

✗ *"She is brave. The text says she went in the cave. This shows bravery."*

✓ *"The character is brave because she faced her fear. For example, the text states, 'She stepped into the cave even though she was scared.' This proves she is brave because she didn't let fear stop her from helping others."*

🛑 7. Copying the Text Instead of Explaining in Their Own Words

Mistake: Some students **copy entire sentences** from the passage instead of summarizing or paraphrasing.

✅ How to Fix It:

- Teach students to **put text evidence in their own words** before writing it down.
- Use **"Think-Pair-Share"** activities where students explain evidence **orally** before writing.

💡 Example:

✗ *"The text says, 'The girl walked into the cave to find her dog.'"*

✓ *"The story shows the girl's bravery because she entered the dark cave to rescue her lost pet."*

📌 Final Takeaways: How to Improve R.A.C.E. Responses

✔ **Check for all four parts**—Restate, Answer, Cite, Explain.

✔ **Use transition words** to connect ideas smoothly.

✔ **Choose strong, relevant evidence** that directly supports the answer.

✔ **Explain why the evidence matters**—don't just list facts.

✔ **Write in a clear, complete sentence**, not just a short response.

Would you like a **checklist** or **student-friendly examples** to help avoid these mistakes? 😊

Notes

Chapter 8:
Fun Activities to Reinforce Learning

- R.A.C.E. method games
- Group activities and writing challenges
- Printable worksheets and templates

Fun At-Home Activities to Reinforce the R.A.C.E. Method

Practicing the **R.A.C.E. method** (Restate, Answer, Cite, Explain) at home doesn't have to feel like homework—it can be fun! Here are some **engaging, hands-on activities** that families can do together to build strong writing skills.

🎲 1. R.A.C.E. Response Game (Roll & Write) 🎲

✅ **How to Play:**

- Grab a **die** and assign each number to a step in R.A.C.E.:
    - 🎲 1-2 = **Restate**
    - 🎲 3-4 = **Answer**
    - 🎲 5 = **Cite Evidence**
    - 🎲 6 = **Explain**
- Read a **short article, story, or paragraph** together.
- Roll the die and **write a response using the step that matches the roll**.
- Keep rolling until you complete the full R.A.C.E. response!

💡 Example:

Read a passage about space exploration.

Question: *Why is space exploration important?*

- 🎲 Roll 2 → Restate: *Space exploration is important because it helps us learn about the universe.*

- 🎲 Roll 4 → Answer: *It allows scientists to discover new planets and understand Earth better.*

- 🎲 Roll 5 → Cite: *For example, the Mars Rover has collected soil samples to study life on Mars.*

- 🎲 Roll 6 → Explain: *This proves that space exploration helps humans prepare for the future and learn about our world.*

🔀 **Variation:** Play with multiple players and have each person add to the response!

🎭 2. R.A.C.E. Acting Challenge 🎭

✅ How to Play:

- Write different **R.A.C.E. questions** on slips of paper and put them in a bowl.

- One person **draws a question** and **acts out** a response while others guess what step they're showing.

- Example: If acting out **Cite Evidence**, they might pretend to read from a book and point to a "quote."

- After acting, work together to write a complete R.A.C.E. response.

💡 **Example Question:** *How does teamwork help people succeed?*

🎭 **Acting Prompt for "Cite"**: Pretend to read from a book and say, *"The story says, 'By working together, the team won the championship.'"*

📌 **Variation:** Turn it into a **charades-style game** where others have to guess the R.A.C.E. step!

📄 3. R.A.C.E. Scavenger Hunt 🔍

✅ **How to Play:**

- Choose a **short story, news article, or passage** to read together.
- Hide four **sticky notes** labeled **R, A, C, and E** around the house.
- After reading, send kids to **find the notes** and complete each step of R.A.C.E. on them.
- Once all four notes are complete, put them together to make a full response!

💡 **Example Question:** *Why is kindness important?*

🔍 **Restate:** *Kindness is important because it helps people feel valued.*

🔍 **Answer:** *It makes the world a better place when people are kind to each other.*

🔍 **Cite:** *For example, the story says, 'Liam shared his lunch with his friend who forgot his food.'*

🔍 **Explain:** *This proves that small acts of kindness can make someone's day better.*

📌 **Variation:** Do this outside and have kids tape their answers to trees, chairs, or walls as they find them!

📺 4. R.A.C.E. Movie or TV Show Night 🏠

✅ How to Play:

- Watch a **favorite movie, TV show, or even a YouTube video** together.
- Pick an important question about the story.
- Use **R.A.C.E. to answer the question** in a written or spoken response.

💡 **Example Question for a Superhero Movie:** *How does the main character show bravery?*

🎬 Response:

- **Restate:** *The main character shows bravery in the movie by facing danger to save others.*
- **Answer:** *Even when he was scared, he took action to protect his city.*
- **Cite:** *For example, in the scene where the villain attacks, the hero stands his ground despite being outnumbered.*
- **Explain:** *This proves that bravery isn't about being fearless but about doing the right thing even when afraid.*

 Variation: Do a **family debate** where each person picks a different example of bravery and defends it using R.A.C.E.!

📝 5. R.A.C.E. Comic Strip Challenge 🎨

✅ How to Play:

- Give kids a **blank comic strip template** or have them fold a paper into **four boxes**.
- Each box represents a step in **R.A.C.E.**

- Instead of writing, **draw a mini-comic** for each part of the response.

💡 **Example Question:** *How does the main character learn a lesson in the story?*

✏️ **Panel 1:** Draw the **question restated** in a thought bubble.

✏️ **Panel 2:** Show the **answer** in a speech bubble.

✏️ **Panel 3:** Draw a book, screen, or sign for **citing evidence**.

✏️ **Panel 4:** Show a character thinking and explaining the answer.

📌 **Variation:** Use **stick figures or emojis** for younger kids!

📢 6. R.A.C.E. Family Debate Night 👥

✅ **How to Play:**

- Pick a fun **discussion topic** (example: "Should kids have longer recess?").
- One person asks a question, and everyone must **answer using R.A.C.E.**
- Each person **writes or says their response**, and the family votes on the best one!

💡 **Example Debate Question:** *Should pets be allowed in school?*

🧩 **Restate & Answer:** *Pets should be allowed in school because they help students feel calm and happy.*

📖 **Cite:** *For example, studies show that therapy animals reduce stress in students.*

💡 **Explain:** *This proves that having pets in school can create a positive learning environment.*

📌 **Variation:** Assign a **judge** (parent or sibling) to **grade responses** and pick the most persuasive argument!

Final Takeaways: Why At-Home R.A.C.E. Activities Work

☑ They make writing fun!

☑ They help kids apply R.A.C.E. naturally in conversations.

☑ They reinforce critical thinking skills.

☑ They create family bonding time while improving literacy.

Chapter 9:
Fiction & Nonfiction Reading Passages and Writing Prompts

Practice Instructions:

- On a separate sheet of paper.
- Restate the question in your own words.
- Answer the question clearly.
- Cite at least one piece of evidence from the passage.
- Explain how the evidence supports your answer.

📖 Fiction Passage 1: The Lost Pencil

Text:

Jaden sat at his desk, searching frantically through his backpack. "Where is it?" he whispered. Today was the big spelling test, and Jaden couldn't find his lucky pencil. It was red with silver stars and had helped him feel confident all year. "Are you okay?" his teacher asked. Jaden nodded slowly, though he felt nervous. Suddenly, his friend Lila tapped him and handed him a pencil. "You dropped this in the hallway," she smiled. Jaden grinned—his lucky pencil was back. He took a deep breath and started the test.

Prompt:

Why was Jaden nervous at the beginning of the story?

📖 Nonfiction Passage 1: Why Bees Matter

Text:

Bees are tiny insects, but they play a huge role in the world. Bees help flowers grow by carrying pollen from one plant to another. This process is called pollination. Without bees, many fruits and vegetables would not grow well. Farmers and scientists are working together to protect bees, because fewer bees mean less food for people and animals.

Prompt:

Why are bees important to plants and people?

📖 Fiction Passage 2: Game Day Trouble

Text:

Maya had practiced soccer every day after school. She was finally ready for the big game. But on the day of the match, storm clouds covered the sky. Rain began to pour. The coach called the game off. Maya sighed but smiled. "There's always next week," she said. She knew all that practice would still help her improve.

Prompt:

How did Maya handle the disappointment when the game was canceled?

📓 Nonfiction Passage 2: The Fastest Land Animal

Text:

The cheetah is the fastest animal on land. It can run up to 70 miles per hour for short distances. Cheetahs use their speed to catch prey like antelopes. Their slim bodies and long tails help them balance and move quickly. Unlike lions or tigers, cheetahs usually hunt during the day.

Prompt:

What makes cheetahs good hunters?

📖 Fiction Passage 3: Sam's Science Fair

Text:

Sam worked hard on his volcano project. He built it from clay and painted it red and black. On the day of the science fair, Sam poured in the baking soda and vinegar. The volcano erupted with fizz! The crowd cheered, and Sam felt proud. Even though he didn't win first place, he knew he had done his best.

Prompt:

How did Sam feel about his science fair project, and why?

Chapter 10:
Worksheets

Worksheet 1: Graphic Organizer

Step   **Notes**

R - Restate _____

A - Answer   _____

C - Cite   _____

E - Explain _____

Worksheet 2: Sentence Starters

Restate: The question is asking about...

I think the question means...

Answer: I believe the answer is...

My answer is...

Cite: For example, the text says...

In the passage, it states...

Explain: This shows that...

This means that...

Worksheet 3: Self-Check Checklist

- ☐ Did I restate the question?
- ☐ Did I clearly answer it?
- ☐ Did I cite evidence from the text?
- ☐ Did I explain how the evidence supports my answer?
- ☐ Did I check for complete sentences and punctuation?

Worksheet 4: R.A.C.E. Practice Sheet

Prompt:

_____

_____

Restate:

_____

_____

Answer:

_____

_____

Cite:

_____

_____

Explain:

_____

_____

Worksheet 5: Color-Code the R.A.C.E.

Directions: Read the paragraph and use different colors to underline each R.A.C.E. part.

- Blue = Restate
- Green = Answer
- Yellow = Cite
- Red = Explain

Paragraph:

_____

_____

_____

_____

_____

_____

_____

_____

Worksheet 6: R.A.C.E. Puzzle Match

Directions: Match the sentence to the correct R.A.C.E. step.

Sentence   R / A / C / E

"The passage shows that…"   _____

"I believe the answer is…"   _____

"This means that…"   _____

"The question is asking…"   _____

Worksheet 7: Peer Review Checklist

Use this checklist to review a classmate's response. Put a ✔ or ✗.

_____ The response restates the question.

_____ The answer is clear and complete.

_____ At least one piece of evidence is cited.

_____ The explanation connects the evidence to the answer.

_____ The response uses correct punctuation and grammar.

Worksheet 8: R.A.C.E. Story Starters

Choose a prompt and complete the R.A.C.E. response:

1. What is your favorite season and why?
2. Should students wear uniforms to school?
3. What is the best pet to have?
4. Why is it important to help others?

Use the following spaces:

Restate:

_____

_____

Answer:

_____

_____

Cite:

_____

_____

Explain:

_____

_____

About the Author

Dr. Yvonne McCowen is an **international best-selling author, publisher, and dedicated educator** who knows firsthand the struggles of writing. As a young African American student, she often found writing assignments frustrating and overwhelming—until she discovered the **R.A.C.E. method**. This simple, structured approach transformed her confidence, turning her into a stronger writer, a better student, and eventually, an inspiring teacher.

With over two decades of experience in education, Dr. McCowen has helped countless students **master writing skills, to think critically, and express themselves clearly**. Now, as a **renowned literacy advocate**, she is on a mission to empower young writers worldwide through engaging books, practical strategies, and accessible learning tools.

Through her writing, publishing, and teaching, she continues to inspire students, educators, and parents to embrace the power of structured, confident writing. To Book for PD's or school visits contact Dr. Yvonne McCowen at drmccowen0921@gmail.com or call 737-228-3207

Bibliography

Graham & Hebert, (2011). Writing to Read: A Meta-Analysis of the Impact of Writing and Writing Instruction on Reading.

National Center for Education Statistics, (2012). NAEP National Assessment of Educational Progress Writing Report.

www.ingramcontent.com/pod-product-compliance
Lightning Source LLC
Chambersburg PA
CBHW061740070526
44585CB00024B/2759